W9-BQU-054

Acts of Attention: The Poems of D.H. Lawrence

In The Fourth World: Poems

The Madwoman in the Attic:
The Woman Writer and the 19th Century Literary Imagination
(co-authored with Susan Gubar)

Shakespeare's Sisters:
Feminist Essays on Women Poets
(co-edited with Susan Gubar)

EMILY'S BREAD

EMILY'S BREAD

POEMS BY

SANDRA M. GILBERT

W · W · NORTON & COMPANY · NEW YORK · LONDON

Copyright © 1984 by Sandra M. Gilbert
All rights reserved.
Published simultaneously in Canada by Stoddart, a subsidiary of General
Publishing Co. Ltd , Don Mills, Ontario.
Printed in the United States of America.

The text of this book is composed in Electra, with
display type set in Goudy Old Style. Composition and
manufacturing by The Maple-Vail Book Manufacturing Group.
Book design by Lilly Langotsky

First Edition

Library of Congress Cataloging in Publication Data

Gilbert, Sandra M.
   Emily's bread.

   I. Title.
PS3557.I34227E4   1984   811'.54   83–19487

ISBN 0-393-01849-0

ISBN 0-393-30150-8 (pbk.)

W. W. Norton & Company, Inc.
500 Fifth Avenue, New York, N.Y. 10110
W. W. Norton & Company Ltd.
37 Great Russell Street, London WC1B 3NU

1 2 3 4 5 6 7 8 9 0

FOR SUSAN GUBAR

with Love and Friendship

CONTENTS

Acknowledgments

Some of the poems in this collection have appeared in periodicals and anthologies, as follows:

The Antioch Review: "Daguerreotype: Wet Nurse"

The Beloit Poetry Journal: "Her House," "Minus Tide"

Beyond Baroque / NewLetters: "Emily's Bread"

Chowder Review: "Daguerreotype: Governess"

Cedar Rock: "Still Life: Woman, Window, Staircase," "Parable of the Clothes"

College English: "Still Life: Woman Cooking"

Contemporary Women Poets: An Anthology: "Still Life: Woman in Blue 'Designer' Dress, Beige Pantihose, White Italian Shoes"

The Cornell Review: "Still Life: Woman in Frog Mask," "Still Life: Old Woman with Apples," "Evening / Mirror / Poem"

Epos: "Daguerreotype: 'Fallen' Woman"

The Massachusetts Review: "Bas Relief: Bacchante"

The Nation: "Snapshot: Nurse," "Glass"

Networks: An Anthology of Bay Area Women Poets: "Daguerreotype: Lace Maker"

New Letters: "Anna La Noia," "Brahms: Symphony #1"

Open Places: "On Black Point Beach," "The Kitchen Dream"

Poetry: "For the Muses," "Sculpture: Naiad / Fountain," "Elegy" (reprinted in *The Poetry Anthology*), "Indiana: The Invitation," "History," "In the Forest of Symbols," "Simplicity," "Sitting"

Poetry Northwest: "The Dressmaker's Dummy," "Sonnet: The Ladies' Home Journal," "Scheherazade," "Daphne," "Daguerreotype: Widow," "Film Clip: 'Spinster'," "February," "On the Third Hand," "The Emily Dickinson Black Cake Walk"

Prairie Schooner: "Insomnia Weather," "Landscape: In the Forest"

Southern Poetry Review: "Metastasis"

Streets: "The Dream of the Shop of the Infinite Ought"

13th Moon: "The Night Grandma Died"

Woman Poet: The West: "The Dream Kitchen"

As a baker of excellent bread Emily's reputation was soon
established in the village, where it won her far more respect
than her reputed "learning." The parish clerk, invading her
kitchen on church affairs, or tradesmen delivering goods, observed
her at her bread-trough, kneading the dough. Though awed by her
silence, some of them noticed the book propped up on the kitchen
table at her side, and the little scraps of paper and pencil to hand,
though for what purposes they did not guess until years later
they learned that she wrote, and published, poetry.

—Winifred Gérin, *Emily Brontë*

She makes all the bread for her father only likes
hers & says "& people must have puddings" this *very*
dreamily, as if they were comets—so she makes them.

—Thomas Wentworth Higginson, to
his wife, about Emily Dickinson

I

HER HOUSE

FOR THE MUSES

They said I couldn't find you.
They said because I'm a *she*,
because the *s* in my name blurs my features,
a hiss around my face like uncombed hair,
you wouldn't be interested.

They said my breasts would hinder me,
heavy, hard to carry, with nipples like blinded eyes.
They said the inflatable rubber cell in my belly
would frighten you, and the lips between my legs:
you'd expect me to eat you up!

But I remember you too well.
You were the immigrant aunts I visited
in the suburbs of my childhood,
keeping house with what you'd salvaged
on the long flight from Paris:

diamonds in the linings of your coats,
embroideries from the 1890s,
Egyptian jewelry, a samovar, old
cashmere scarves, a rosewood wardrobe
larger than the bathroom.

Aunt Rose, your hair was black, it grew in wings from your
        forehead.
Aunt Lil, your hair was white, it circled your skull like a shawl.
You see, I remember.
And your fourth-floor flat, where I visited you, where you
fed me oranges and honey, cakes and wine—

I remember that too: the print
of the lovers in the forest, the witch
pictures on the walls, the plants
that hummed in the dark, the
black feet of the peacock.

You spoke to me there, you told me the stories.
I was yours as much as any boy.
Or more: for the notion of my breasts was yours,
you planned them, you designed them.
And the afternoon you led me to the rosewood wardrobe

and opened the great carved door
you smiled when I myself pulled out the center drawer,
smiled when all that light came spilling out
and wrapped itself around my arms, my thighs, my shoulders
like a bolt of old satin.

"A mantle, not a shroud," you said.

THE DREAM KITCHEN

Her eyes glowed pale as radium.
She said: "Well, if you're good
I'll let you come into
the dream kitchen. . . ."

I was demure. Plaid skirt,
white anklets, gold barrette,
clasped hands always before me
like the hands of the dead.

She said: "Well?"
                    and I followed her
through the tall door,
and the dream kitchen

with its pulsing ovens
rose around us like a mountain range,
the dream kitchen held us in fleshy
silence, the dream kitchen

rocked us, stroked us,
streaming with syrups and creams
and soupy hollows.
"Check out the cupboards,"

she said. "Open the drawers.
The place is all yours."
I pulled a throbbing handle: streaks of cutlery.
Another: platters inscribed "I'm yours."

"Remember your manners."
I turned to thank her,
but she was gone:
I was alone.

My enormous kitchen coughed, trembled,
and began to hum.

THE DRESSMAKER'S DUMMY

In my grandmother's room, treasures of old mahogany,
intricate and enigmatic as the 1890s:
the three-paned mirror, the great highboy
with knobs like cabbage roses and expensive brasses,

the bed of generations—brown and black, teak and rosewood,
       inlays
older than I could ever be—and a mattress
soft from half a century of sleepers,
and quilts, and goose feathers,

and cast adrift on the crimson carpet
a dressmaker's dummy, headless, armless,
a barren stork on one steel leg. . . .
The stork that brought me!—for as I grew it grew with me,

its plaster hips were padded to mimic mine,
and when I sprouted breasts so did the dummy,
and as I lengthened it slid up its pole, became lean, became bone,
became my own self, hardening, final,

and at night, through the shadows, I watched it shine
in the mirror, the streetlamps casting white eyes
on its ludicrous height, white scorn on its hips,
its empty neck, its stiff stuck frame:

and still it's there in my grandmother's room,
curved like the prow of a ship, cleaving the air
dumb as a wooden whaler's wife, a hopeless
image of me, frozen and bare,

sailing forward into the triple mirror,
wading waist-deep, a dead lady, into the future.

SONNET: THE LADIES' HOME JOURNAL

The brilliant stills of food, the cozy
glossy, bygone life—mashed potatoes
posing as whipped cream, a neat mom
conjuring shapes from chaos, trimming the flame—
how we ached for all that,
that dance of love in the living room,
those paneled walls, that kitchen golden
as the inside of a seed: how we leaned
on those shiny columns of advice,
stroking the *thank yous*, the firm thighs, the wise
closets full of soap.
                     But even then
we knew it was the lies we loved, the lies
we wore like Dior coats, the clean-cut airtight
lies that laid out our lives in black and white.

PINK

The inside walls of the shell are pink and unused.
No cracks, no hangings.
Here the yolk sleeps.
Here the chromosomes are silent:
they have not yet learned their own language.
Then what are the swayings, the hidden scuffles?

Something pecks, here and there.
Pecks, twists, frets.
Some shadow of the world
haunts the egg
the way the dangers of vermilion
threaten pink.

EVENING/MIRROR/POEM

Spiegel. . . . Ihr, noch das leeren Salles Verschwender. . . .
—R. M. Rilke, *Die Sonette an Orpheus*

Evening. Drop by drop of darkness,
the empty hall drains into the mirror

as if misty lips were sucking it in,
or as if the cold glass were really a cliff edge

over which every image must fall
in a sweet slow-motion tumble—

first the hat rack, then the hall table,
then the unlit chandelier, the hats and coats,

the rubber plant, the ferns, the African violets,
and last the Persian carpet

with its angelic blue, its red
vivid as desert heat. . . .

Midnight. Darkness. The pure
threads shred, the colors falter:

and the drowned eyes of the weaver
stare into the space where the mirror was,

sexy and impassive
as Narcissus.

PARABLE OF THE CLOTHES

Five A.M. The clothes scratch like animals
at the belly of the dryer.
They long to be free.
To be born again, in a life without buttons!

Whirling, they meditate, discard
the lint of memory.
Shall the threads be untied?
Will the seams give way?

Some doubt, some heap themselves in corners, wondering.
Which came first, the cloth or the pattern?
Is the soul merely a jacket?
In the cold wash of dawn

one pale shirt
sets sail across cold fields,
its elbows filling with mist,
its collar undone.

HER HOUSE

1

At night, in the dark,
she sucks on thoughts of it:
square and brown, it's her sugar cube,
her love, her all-night lolly,
four grainy walls and a crimson carpet
to lull her to sleep,
whispering
someday we'll be yours
to keep, to keep. . . .

2

Two mice in a cage
going round and round;
where one is hidden
one is found.

Three mice in a cage,
leaping, leaping.
One eats, one sleeps,
one does the keeping.

Four mice in a cage,
dancing, prancing.
One eats, one sleeps,
one's romancing,

and one is weeping, weeping. . . .

3

She says: "They speak of the House of Atreus,
why not the House of Hilda,
the House of Angela,
the House of Mary,
the House of Artemis?"

4

Dear God! One day she opened
the pantry door and saw
the sea beating among the cupboards,
its webs of brine tangled
like fine white linen
where the cups once were.

5

The House of Hilda is a broom closet.
Angela's House is a waxy bell
like the bowl of a lily.
But the House of Artemis (she decides)
is slim, glittering, almost invisible—
a green needle stitching and unstitching
the borders of the forest,
the hems of light.

6

This is too Female (he said).
Effeminate, your basic
Earth Mother Number,
or else your fundamental

Furies bit—Norns, Fates,
all that.
        He laughed,
for O he was a whiskery cynic.

When a great green paw
slid from the fleshy earth pit
and batted him into blackest shadows
as if he were a silly pebble,
he hardly noticed:
he declared that, in his profundity,
he could no longer tell night from day.

7

After twenty years she daydreams
she's wading through a carpet of blood.
At night, the long thin sharp
tongue of the dark
licks every drop
up.

8

Thirty years. The house swells, bulges, rocks
like the head and belly of a
Disney madman,
or like a great balloon
straining to rise, to rise and
break its ties
with the weedy, buzzing, taking-
off place.

9

She wakes in the pearly sweat of
just before dawn: the long sea receding
beneath her bedroom window
leaves a lawn wet with moonlight
and the beached bleached ribs
of one more question: *fifty?*
(Years? Months? Minutes?)
She pads downstairs in a hissing silence, thinking
What will I find now
in my kitchen?

And, truly, the forest has made its way
in and out of her oven: foxes
in the breakfast nook, mice
beside the sugar bowl,
mosquitoes droning, moths flittering,
clicking and scrabbling of shadows,
twining, untwining of branches,
clattering, twittering, rustling:

the House of Artemis, she thinks,
unstitching itself,
as if somewhere
in some tremulous wine-stained dream
the animal goddess in her skull
had heard a woodland horn blow

and seen the loved walls fall. . . .

ON THE THIRD HAND

On the one hand
I am afraid. I wear a school ring.
I prick my tender fingers, remember typewriters,
        carry hammers.

On the other hand
I believe there's nothing to fear.
I wear a wedding ring. I have pink fingernails.
        My skin is soft as vanilla cream.

On the third hand
I wear the rings of crystal and pollen
and the rings the Etruscans fashioned
from feathers, auguries, seeds, and
        salts of strange origin:

these rings murmur in the dark,
murmur and click in foreign tongues,
keeping my cold third hand awake,
promising pleasures unique as fingerprints,
pains closer to bone than skin.

The fingers of my third hand are green,
they are yellow and green.
Someone gave them to me in a dream
when I was twenty-nine.

With the third hand
I write letters to the world of glass,

letters instantly read and memorized
by missionaries of the light, letters swallowed
by emptiness, letters conveyed by silent messengers
    to polar silences. (Somewhere
    in other words, they are well known.)

    On the third hand
I play the piano of grass, and looped around cold fingers
I carry the green keys that unlock the door in the oak
    behind which my great aunts live smiling
    in a parlor lined with glittering samovars:

    with the third hand
    I turn all the handles, and once again
    the ancient tea steams out like rain.

I I

DAGUERREOTYPES

EMILY'S BREAD

1857   *Emily's bread won a prize at the annual Cattle Show.*
1858   *Emily served as a judge in the Bread Division of the Cattle Show.*
                              —John Malcolm Brinnin, "Chronology,"
                                  Selected Poems of Emily Dickinson

Inside the prize-winning blue-ribbon loaf of bread,
there is Emily, dressed in white,
veiled in unspeakable words,
not yet writing letters to the world.

No, now she is the bride of yeast,
the wife of the dark of the oven,
the alchemist of flour, poetess of butter,
stirring like a new metaphor in every bubble

as the loaf begins to grow.
Prosaic magic, how it swells,
like life, expanding, browning
at the edges, hardening.

Emily picks up her pen, begins to scribble.
Who'll ever know? "This is my letter
to the world, that never. . . ."
Lavinia cracks an egg, polishes

the rising walls with light. Across
the hall the judges are making notes:
firmness, texture, size, flavor.
Emily scribbles, smiles. She knows it is

the white aroma of her baking skin
that makes the bread taste good.
Outside in the cattle pen the blue-ribbon heifers
bellow and squeal. Bread means nothing to them.

They want to lie in the egg-yellow sun.
They are tired of dry grain, tired of grooming and love.
They long to eat the green old meadow
where they used to live.

DAGUERREOTYPE: GOVERNESS

She comes toward us like a troublesome memory,
carrying her basket of *maybes*, her clergyman's umbrella,
her grandfather, her clergyman, her large gold watch
in the shape of a decaying apple.

Her eyes are darning needles, her breasts pincushions.
Between her thighs, icy as panes of glass,
a thin ribbon of silk flutters and cries.
There are no strong verbs in her sentences

because there is no skin on the back of her hands.
There is no end to her paragraphs
because her fingers are tipped with the shivering wings
of tiny insects—moths, beetles, stingless bees.

Four children are attached like yo-yos to her knees.
On her head she wears a feathered hat, dark as a beard.
She tells us she'd like to go back to the parsonage
with its kitchen of apples, its dim windows, its stony orchard.

She misses the hoops in the garden, she says, and the shells,
and the wise silence of the stuffed parrot.
If she cannot return, she explains, she would like to die.
If she cannot die, she will accept her life

as the most expedient solution.
Behind her we see the shape of a large trunk or bureau.
For some reason, it seems clear
she stores little vials of her mother's blood in there.

DAGUERREOTYPE: "FALLEN" WOMAN

The clock between her thighs ticks like a heart of gold:
satins, furbelows, no matter what she wears
she knows it's there, quick treasure, time machine that carries her,
pink nymph of the *pavé*,
from mattress to mattress, day to day.

Rustling her colors, she tells us this
between gulps of beer,
confides, "It's the drink that gets me through,"
grins, twitches her skirt. Her hair
is a curious shade of green

(from spit and sweat, she thinks)
and clings like fingers to her neck;
her frayed shawl, dull as a night's work,
sways around her hips; her breasts are question marks.
Some afternoons she sleeps, she says, and dreams,

green ringlets in her eyes,
that she's a tree, falling through the Thames,
falling through the easy mud,
into Australia, where the sun is hot
and an armless man sucks out her hole, her clock, her heart.

DAGUERREOTYPE: WET NURSE

Everything about her thick—thick wrists, thick ankles,
skin thick as felt—she dawdles
through the rich man's nursery,
stupid, staring at nothing, wearing her heavy body
idly as the heifer wears her bell.

When the silk-skinned child stirs and whimpers
in its slim mahogany stall,
she yawns, offers a nipple thick as cheese,
hot as the haystacks where she lies in dreams,
legs spread to country lovers.

Rocking and dozing, oozing juice, she says
she still remembers the other child,
the wailing one she left in the suburbs
to be weaned on tea or water.
It had, she thinks, red down

on its wobbly head; or was it brown?
She sleeps. The child sucks, gurgles,
also sleeps. Behind thick lids
we see her pupils flicker, back and forth.
A small vein pulses in her neck, while

from somewhere far inside her breast, her skull,
rises the humming of an insect self, thin, elegant,
spinning a web of bitter milk
to drown the mild
breathing of the rich man's child.

DAGUERREOTYPE: WIDOW

For thirty years now she's lived
in the little village of Extremity,
that dull village where the language is Hanging On,
a language of silence, small wheels, ruts in the road,
a language heavy with shutters and ruined walls,
each noun a bottomless dry well.

Back from her walk in the mountains, caped
in the smell of the sour grass she gathers daily,
she stares at us, chin fixed
and square as patience, lips the shape
of a dried fruit that was once a smile.
Over one arm she carries a basket of pebbles:

these grow like mushrooms in her garden,
these are her livelihood, each night
she sorts them by color and weight,
and fashions them into talisman rings
for the women in the soft valleys,
the children, the mourners.

At dawn, she tells us, she paces
the small square in the center of her village,
alert as any sentry.
The bells stutter their reveille
and she paces, paces, corner to corner.
It's so hot in this town, so dusty,

even the mountains are flaking away.
And what if the pebble harvest should vanish
like the windows, the acorns, the silk?
The leaves have long since flown from the trees;
the chickens leap toward the teeth of the fox;
the cow lies down and weeps in her milk.

DAGUERREOTYPE: LACE MAKER

From days spent bending over the pattern,
eyes and fingers caught in the tightening
mazes of the lace,
she has assumed the shape
of a hook, its deft ferocity,
thin glitter and abstraction.

She stares into the camera, very old,
no children now, no stewpots, never a berrying
afternoon with sun like pure hot iron
at her back, nothing but a shawl
on her shoulders now, black and thick:
and her eyes, passionate hooks,

say *only the lace, the lace is left,*
only the white paths, the stitches like steps
in a dance whose meaning is still unknown,
the walls of thread impossible to cross,
the tiny corners, the fields of webs and flowers,
the serious knotting and unknotting at the end.

BAS RELIEF: BACCHANTE

She's not at all as we expected, wearing
(instead of oiled breasts, a torn toga, a sexy swoon)
a sort of fur ruff and the calm look
of those animal-headed judges, wise as roots,
who rule the world below.

They were the ones, she says, who watched when Orpheus,
that show-off, gave the look that kills
to Eurydice on the stony path.
Betrayed girl-bride, stuck halfway up the hill
and halfway down!

            Her fur ruff twitches
as she makes this case. It's clear
she never liked the bastard anyway,
the swaggering bastard with his silver flute,
precious proboscis, mean baton,

commanding silence, silence from everyone,
shutting the trees up, quieting the wind
and the quick birds, and the women.
Without his manly anthems,
everything, she says, would sing, would sing.

As she speaks, a furry feathery humming
rises from the stones she stands on
and we see she's after all a lioness,
serenely hungry to dismember him.
But behind her, hidden among leaves,

dressed in a gauzy apron, a crinoline, a rhinestone necklace,
there is Isis, that apple blossom queen,
that silly sister-in-law,
that superintendent of nurses,
ready as ever to pick up the bloody pieces.

SCULPTURE: NAIAD/FOUNTAIN

Stone faced, living always in water,
feeling always the pulse of water,
its dazzling thickness, shape, weight, power,

how is she to say the sentence
that curls like a fern around her lips?
Consider: at night, while you sleep on feathers,

she is still in the cold heartbeat,
the veils of clarity shifting before her eyes
like panes of ice, keen, murderous.

Legless, rooted to that blind center
where the water churns, murmurs, prepares
its terrifying leap upward,

she's forgotten the warm stream where she swam
that afternoon the sculptor captured her,
forgotten nipples and milk, fingertips and leaves,

and everything except the waiting, the white sound,
and the beat, the colorless engine beat
that explodes *over, around,* and again, *over, around,*

caging her in thinness,
in light that praises and denies,
in the gasping alien measure

of the sculptor's breath.
Do you wonder if she dreams of death?
Turning in your sleep, shut eyes moving in the dark,

do you imagine her return to the river of her girlhood,
where sun and shade shape the water
and she pioneers, shouting, to the current's mouth?

You wake and look: she's still here,
fixed in the blank piazza, which has
no words to ease the violence of her silence.

III

METASTASIS

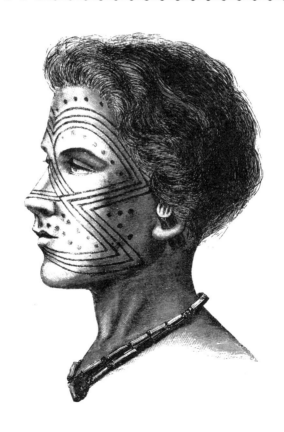

ELEGY

The pages of history open. The dead enter.
It is winter in the spine of the book
where they land, inexplicable texts,
and a small rain falling, a mist of promises,
disjointed sentences, woes, failures.

The dead are puzzled:
was it for this they left
the land of grammar, the syntax of their skin?
We turn the pages. We read.
Sometimes, in moments of vertigo,

we notice that they're speaking.
Tiny whinings and murmurings arise,
as of insects urging their rights, their dissatisfactions,
invisible insects dwelling uncomfortably
in the margins, in the white spaces around words.

ANNA LA NOIA

La mano le luceva che mi porse.   .   .   .
   —G. Ungaretti, *"Alla Noia"*

She was the sister I never had,
a pale Italian girl from the dry, olive-gray
hills of Tuscany—
  Anna La Noia
  Anna Ennui
with eyes like seeds
focusing hard and sharp
on a darkness I couldn't see.

At dawn she appeared
in a white shift
like a novice, a nurse's aide
beside my bed:
  high milkless breasts, high child's voice,
  cool skin, indifferent wrists.   .   .   .

We gossiped in the early heat,
made up old stories, poems, lies:
in the half-light
that leaked around the shutters
she held out a shining hand—
  Anna La Noia
  Anna Ennui.   .   .   .
I pressed my lips against small
knuckles cold as pebbles.

What was it I remembered then?
Now, what have I forgotten?

All morning, straying, whispering
under the hard green olives
she led me on:
      her tender neck, her rosy vulnerable
      schoolgirl knees!

At noon in the simmering vineyard
we embraced,
we became one woman.

INSOMNIA WEATHER

Outside the night rolls by like a freight train,
unreeling car after car of darkness
as if a rare disease invaded the sky.

Next door my doctor sleeps in the silver
ear of his stethoscope. His hasty breath
slams through the air like the blade of a buzz saw,

cutting through bone, cutting through tangled lines
of family connections—a wife with earrings
that pierce the pillow, three children

who hang like phones on the hooks of his life,
an aged mother who rocks in her sleep
and dreams of her son the doctor.

And I, I turn in my bed and dream
of the doctor whose breath cannot heal.
A needle of wind flickers between us.

The garden is black, its branches clatter, sicken,
watching black clouds thunder past,
links on a chain, tornado express.

FEBRUARY

The oak leaves open, bitter, succulent,
with sharp thin edges keen as tiny teeth—
green lives, alive in the blue smog,
green teeth, biting the bitter sky.

February already, and a haze portending blossoms
thickens the garden air, and I'm asked
to review poems, somebody thinks
I might be an authority

so stacks of earnest books lie on my desk
passive as necks on a chopping-block,
tender as baby skin—too vulnerable!—and I begin
by sharpening pencils, yawning, breathing slow,

and then I'm pleased, then angry; breathing fast
I scribble wickedness in margins, fall past
clumps of words like Satan, Siva, shaking fists,
desiring for myself the tall blue throne,

destroyer, arbiter, myself alone. And then
I land in thorny branches, hug
my infant wit, my cold crown,
and see that I myself am February,

bitter, mean, biting the sky with hard green teeth,
hungry for everyone's skin,
waiting not very patiently for some March
of great white blossoms to begin.

THE DREAM OF THE SHOP
OF THE INFINITE OUGHT

Down three stone steps I stumble
into the dust-colored shop of the Infinite Ought.

Evening. Breaths of night spilling into the room.
Just one clerk left, dark suited, wan.

We're closing up. His pale voice rises
from a table stacked with books, books

multiply like shadows as the night pours in:
the darker it gets the more I think I've seen.

It's closing time, he murmurs, and an iron
gate slides shut, grillwork curved like an alphabet.

I cry, *My God, please open that!*
I've got to go. I never wanted to buy books anyhow.

Bland as his suit
he opens the gate,

and up the three stone steps I flee
and down the long blank evening street.

Sheet metal clanging in the wind,
the shop sign swings: *Infinite Ought.*

What have I left behind, what phrase, what thought?
I turn to look and spy him in the street—

dark tie, white shirt, shadowy overcoat,
walking at his steady, tired shopman's pace,

deliberate and calm,
faster than I can run.

HISTORY

—*For Christina Le May*

May Day. Fifth Avenue. 1982.
Bag ladies hunch toward me on legs like broken
tree trunks, stumps of other selves, while
limber guerrillas with walkie-talkies and running shorts
slouch through the crowd,

sun flaps the flags, kids cry, peddlars
hawk mechanical planes, bracelets, scarves, oranges.
"All stolen," murmurs my old high school friend
who has two metal plates in her legs
from the crash last year on Riverside and 81st.

I think of Denise last week, breathless in Palo Alto
about the coming nuclear holocaust
as we stroll past Bonwit's,
where plaster ladies pose in thigh-high ruffles—
"Do we have to pay to *look?*" my friend inquires—

and I think how twenty-five years ago
we wandered through the Village—yellow
slickers, smooth chignons, yellow
flowers at our throats—
and just here, at 57th, as the walkie-talkies mutter by,

new yellow tulips thieve the light
and a wandering woman, thick fingered, gray,
stoops and steals a bunch
to stuff in her crumpled Bonwit's bag
beside tissue paper, cornflakes, last night's half-eaten hot dog.

THE NIGHT GRANDMA DIED

Adrift on the pillows. "She just died," said the nurse.
"A heart attack," the doctor said.
"It was easy, peaceful," I told her daughter.

I tried to picture the pincers of heaven
reaching down and twitching her, a little wrinkled diamond,
from the sweet white cot she lay on.

Tears and sniffles. My consolation
didn't work. Not even for me.
What was it, in the end, that wouldn't go away?

The bed. The feel of the cold rails
sliding up and down when people came with needles,
the gray rails grating, clanking, her fingers

yearning toward them like a baby's lips,
hoping for suction. And the white sheets
stiff as sails, scraping skin as if skin were wind, insubstantial.

And the night light, flashing, going out, flashing again.
And the tough mattress, sullen as a shark's back,
rising toward the nurse's hands

on its steel track.

FOR MY AUNT IN MEMORIAL HOSPITAL

Mid-October. A warm moist day.
The sorrow of the trees, burning
toward winter, flares in the air,
each leaf a little rocket crackling out.

But where you are, nothing burns, nothing blooms.
They've emptied your body of its enemies,
they're filling you with sterile juices.
From your sealed window on the fourteenth floor

you see blank sky, smoke, the doped profile
of a stone forest. Mourning my trees,
I imagine you lying in the silence that leaks
like ether from the corridors:

you imagine nothing, you try to smile.
My leaves crackle and fall.
Your forest is still, the growth of a gray day.
I believe you are waiting for me.

METASTASIS

At the cancer hotel, a lobby full of artificial plants,
leaves in the sane green shapes of health,
historical leaves mimicking the past—
and tubes blooming from groins, noses, armpits,
and starved faces in the dayroom
on every floor, thin images
reflecting the clean sheen of the ceiling. . . .

"Just lie down, honey." The nurse's aide,
indifferent as a bellboy, sells the new patient
on a quiet corner. This is it. The last resort.
"Here's your water. Here's your buzzer."
The patient bobs, a courteous guest,
patient, never shows displeasure.
Looking east, over the river, her cousin

watches jets spurt toward Florida, California:
"Kennedy? LaGuardia?" she wonders,
but the patient never turns, never answers.
Unpacking herself like a suitcase,
she sorts, plans, rearranges.
Here's the nightgown, there's the bathrobe.
When are the meals? Where's the soap?

Tomorrow she'll carry herself in a plastic bag,
sanitary, disposable, to the recreation room
at the end of the hall. The Magnavox
will smile, a tour director,
and she'll gaze past sealed panes
at the roof of the children's wing
where roots of September flowers—"autumn color"—

writhe in tubs, trying to get out,
and pigeons settle like insect swarms
among the swings and the deck chairs,
calm as travelers pretending not to see
the musty rugs, the infected
piazzas, the unsavory
kitchens of disease.

MINUS TIDE

The sea draws back, her nervous doors
slide open for 5,000 miles,
and we walk out ten extra feet
into the secret places—

vulnerable tide pools, cool
clefts pulsing with anemones,
maternal ponds where dim
cells crawl or scuttle,

each a fleshy pinkish gray, intestinal
and functional: the color of biology,
undecorative, nonmetaphoric,
unself-conscious, *busy*.

Prurient interlopers, we skid across
seaweedy rocks, splash through ocean mud
that's more alive than blood.
My hand clings to my daughter's, my mind

reaches for poems. But
there's no moralizing such an endless body.
Smiling, a Japanese woman passes
with an armful of seaweed and water.

She's going to eat these tangled salt ideas,
before they eat *her*.

IV

STILL LIVES

STILL LIFE: WOMAN COOKING

The spaghetti spins in its cauldron, a tangle of roots,
moon white, writhing under bubbles.

Light pours like milk from the ceiling.
Thyme, oregano, rosemary sharp as needles

make little patterns in the steam.
I divide and measure, pour, sift, strain,

garlic skinning my fingers, onions filling my eyes.
Every night is the feast of tongues, and my oven

full always, my kitchen
plump as a heart,

my cupboards buttery with life.
Only I wonder, sometimes,

what is that white disturbance—
like foam, like hissing—

in the flour bin?
What is the raw branch of darkness

that unfolds itself, morning after morning,
from the cold stove?

What is that song the brook trout sing
as they crackle in the pan?

FILM CLIP: "SPINSTER"

—In memory of M. F. D.

It's raining. She doesn't want to go home.
We promise to watch from the window
to see that she's safe. It rains,
and we watch from behind our house:

her windshield wipers begin to beat—
clack clack, like lunatics.
No one approaches. Rain, trees, sidewalks.
Nothing moves. Nothing talks.

But she idles her car
as if she wishes the engine would die,
and a tall stranger with a face
of Plato, a face of newsprint,

a face of the Marquis de Sade—
and a trench coat, and all that—
would rescue her with cigarettes and cocoa.
She twists her fingers, rolls down the window, cries,

"I'm a shark, I'd like to eat everyone up!"
And we have to listen!
We have to watch
as her hands turn to string, to knots;

watch as her arms fall off,
devoured by shadows,
and her car explodes in the street;
watch as the strange face of Plato

approaches her lips like the glistening snout
of some night animal,
and the teeth of the Marquis de Sade
close around her cold ankle.

She screams "It isn't fair!"
O Plato, the blood is everywhere.

STILL LIFE: WOMAN IN BLUE "DESIGNER" DRESS, BEIGE PANTIHOSE, WHITE ITALIAN SHOES

When I wear this dress
I feel like a fish that has suddenly grown legs,
like a tree compelled to walk on its branches,

like feathers without a body, rowing nowhere,
petals in the Shah's finger bowl,
all edges and icy surfaces.

Mornings I complain to my closet:
"A social convention," the hangers cry
in their voices of iron.

But why these silks through which the wind
sifts incessantly, like sand,
like an angry abrasive?

Why these heels of stone that thicken
the ground I walk on?
I am the oyster whose shell has burst:

there's no pearl inside,
only knees, acres of knees—and cushions—and a new
paste carapace.

O let me go back to the sea,
let me start over again,
disguised as a shark, or a warrior!

SNAPSHOT: NURSE

Midnight. The water ticking into the sink,
each drop a tiny knife that severs time
from time. She watches, wonders what there is

to watch for, watches as her invalid—
breath fading, mask of skin disintegrating—
lapses into his mattress.

She's young, stiff, careful. He's old
and dull as a seal, gray tatters
flung like a curse across the pillow.

What should she fear?
And yet when the clock tolls two
it seems to her his death is everywhere:

the windows rattle with it and the sofa sags,
rugs shred, clocks whir, ceilings
blur and lower, even trees outside the house

bend in the heavy wind surrounding her, as if
the night itself were her patient, long
and slack, and she were

locked into black laborious lungs,
cells thick with some unspoken hate
that will never breathe her out.

STILL LIFE: WOMAN IN FROG MASK

When I wear this mask
I return to the swamp where I was born:
around me there's a seething,
a night that hisses with flowers,
a night of tentacles and buzzing,
a night of shimmering wings through which I swim,
a gleam on the surface, a shudder, a droplet of sweat.

The men at the party regard me gravely:
the prince wonders, *shall I dance with a frog?*
The prime minister is amused.
The two grandfathers dressed as a mule
make clumsy advances, they're shy, they whinny
through cardboard nostrils.
I am indifferent,

for my legs have grown crooked, I've become
an egg sac leaping in mud,
green as a lily pad, green as the great
sexual grin of the waters,
the hot tunnels inside my body.
Let them gallop all night in their cardboard!
I'm floating alone, here in the corner.

After the ball, I'll peel off this face,
expose my bones once more on the cold
table of dreams, and wait for the clear ether, the antiseptic.
Beyond the windows of my room, while I sleep,
dawn will split the black pod of the sky
like a bloody knife.
And I'll come back to myself.

STILL LIFE: WOMAN,
WINDOW, STAIRCASE

If I could swim through this window!
If I could pass like a fish into the green
waters of the night garden!
Out there I imagine the primroses, peonies, clematis

nodding in silence, nodding and groping
like hands on the ocean floor
toward a secret ring:
the prize I desire, the ring at the bottom of darkness,

the ring that shines in the eyes of the trout!
But my children stir in their beds,
my husband's snores rise like balloons,
testing the air: he wants to be sure

I am here, I am here.
When I try to escape,
try to unscrew my arms and legs
and swim out there,

the treads on the stair become teeth,
my house the mouth of a fox
slammed shut around my waist,
the night air rancid with its breath.

LANDSCAPE: IN THE FOREST

Midnight. The witch's hut
splits like a pomegranate.
Dried flowers pour from seams in the wall.
The floorboards shiver, shred, caress
themselves with splintery claws,
pine needles, in love with their own scent.

And now the forest, where only this evening
the coaches of princes clattered,
is silent—the ladies vanished like light,
the fur, the velvet—and now
the witch in her child clothing
wanders among green branches,

her skin the wax of berries, her feathery hair
innocent as new leaves.

STILL LIFE: OLD WOMAN WITH APPLES

I've been walking seventy years
along the path of the apples.
Take them, my grandmother said,
and walk as far as you can, and as hard.

And I did, though I was small, so small,
and they were so big, so cold, so red.
Redder than thunder! Cold red
glands of winter, spilling frost on my road!

Red as the faces that blinked out of windows,
signaling—Girlie! Come *this* way! Come *here*!
My cloak was tiny, a shred of shadow,
but I slipped past the houses, the books, the kettles.

The apples! The apples! *Walk as far as you can, and as hard!*
I walked till my feet became snails,
walked till each apple groaned from my palm, a tree
of bitter bark, straining, immense.

And lately I think the apples have started to speak.
At night, as I creep through the endless
orchard of my hair,
I hear bubbles of sound come from the stems,

and each dawn, crawling the road, I hear
a baying around me, a quickening of voices.
They're circling my head, red planets,
barking, muttering.

Already I taste the secret meaning:
it's a white sugar that coats my tongue,
a trail of ice in my throat
as if I had swallowed a cold seed, or a stone.

LANDSCAPE: PIG FARM, COUNTY GALWAY

5 A.M.
　　　　A sun like a drunken tinker
drags another morning
over the edge of the farm.
Time for tea,

time for the handyman's banquet,
time for the husband's fingers
to poke like hoes
into cringing furrows . . . .
She brushes her hair before a smoky mirror,

blinks, stares, rubs her eyes.
Across the weedy yard
new piglets shriek in their mud pies,
and the old sow groans for breakfast.
Tasks, days, teas:

　　　　　　　　her daughters
scrabble in the kitchen;
her boy creaks in his crib;
on the hills above the farm
the ghosts of philosophers

sit like judges—Heraclitus, Aristotle, uttering
being and nothingness, flux and fixity.
She bends to the breakfast, the pigs, the tea;
the dirt that clots her lashes thickens her boots.
Beyond the hills

it is green and blue, it is sky and stone,
it is Ireland where Maeve the warrior queen
rides through windy tunnels under the world
and the smoke of her sword rises like mist
above the barrows and the pig-black field.

V

The Emily Dickinson
Black Cake Walk

INDIANA: THE INVITATION

Evening. The sky is wondering
   what color next.
(In the highest branches the green's
   still clear and warm,
but under the pines the grass is
   losing its shape.)

Visit me here, where the stream of air
   defines itself
toward darkness, and the roads beyond
   the pine forest
reach through cornfields, through Whitehall and
   Freeman and all

the unmapped dilapidated towns,
   mysterious as
sentences read backward, curved
   like the fingers
of a hand trying to grasp
   the past we never had.

PARACHUTIST

—For Elliot

The wind hisses in my ear as
I drive away, a tigress

purring along the highway.
Leaves and corn, the fields of Indiana

wall me in. They're maps
of where I am—abstract, judicious, calm—

but suddenly a parachute—
a real white parachute!—

comes drifting down, with someone,
I don't know who, its enigmatic cargo.

And then I see it's you!—
you, bland, affable, swaying

on the silky cord,
swaying, bumping, bubbling

back to me: the golden field
receives you like history, a major monument

transported by a vast
upended blossom.

You smile down at me, your ankles sway.
Dear friend, dear General, you're

a monument, yet light as air.
And how long will you stay?

DAPHNE

1   Her father often said to her, "Daughter, you owe me a son-in-law; you owe me grandchildren." She, hating the thought of marriage as a crime, with her beautiful face tinged all over with blushes, threw her arms around her father's neck, and said, "Dearest father, grant me this favour, that I may always remain unmarried, like Diana." He consented, but at the same time said, "Your own face will forbid it."

—*Bulfinch's Mythology*

2

I see it now. This is
how it happened, this is how
the heavy bars of the sun

fell on her: like thick hands
seizing her breasts, her shoulders,
rocking her backward, prying her thighs apart,

announcing the searing tongue
of the intruder—
                    and she ran

or tried to run
on feet suddenly melting and vague,
while the great heat knitted her

into the stones.
Then what was there to do
but make the best of the surprising change,

be glad of charity?
For with the rooting came new shapes:
thighs, losing their softness, fusing

into a round of power;
arms not two but twenty, rising,
stiffening, everywhere

against the god, refusing
to lie still at her sides;
breasts crusted, belly scaled with armor;

and green tongues, tongues of her own
grown over her
in bursts of scorn—

a mane of tongues, flung from her arms!
At first, astonished, how she must have
clattered, hissed, seethed

in her new language: then—
I know this now—
sighing, she relaxed into the whole

of her different shape, felt
the flood of alien blood,
and entered the secret network

of her other self—how far down
the nervous rootings reached, farther
than her tongues could tell!

Swaying, sucking, leaning
into that hidden body,
at last she learned

the truth of the dark eating
that goes on forever,
                        under the ground.

3   Apollo stood amazed. He touched the stem, and felt the flesh
tremble under the new bark. He embraced the branches, and lav-
ished kisses on the wood. The branches shrank from his lips. "Since
you cannot be my wife," said he, "you shall assuredly be my tree. I
will wear you for my crown; I will decorate with you my harp and
my quiver; and when the great Roman conquerors lead up the trium-
phal pomp to the Capitol, you shall be woven into wreaths for their
brows."

—*Bulfinch's Mythology*

SCHEHERAZADE

Night falls, a curtain, no, a catapult,
and her feet are bricks, thick, unwieldy.
It's time again! time to go west on feet of fever,
time to march, brick after brick, rose-flushed

heartbeat after heartbeat,
into the sunset, the red-gold
throne room where he waits,
silent, naked except for his crown

and sceptre:
                    her king, her master, her
listener. She undoes
her corset, she loosens her womb,

she marches in,
soldierly and thin,
to crouch on his knee.
Once upon a time.

(Is she once? Is he time?)
As the saying goes, she tosses her head.
Freer than verse, her dark hair
flows in the darkening room,

and her story comes and streams
round as curls, seductive, sweet,
until he wraps her tail of hair
around her bone-white throat:

Your muffler, darling.
                    And she smiles, kisses,
thinking, bending,
this damned plot has no ending.

PSYCHE

1

Night after night the embrace of darkness,
the voice that whispers *you are the chosen one*, the hot
phallus of shadow, entering, entering. . . .

2

She lies alone in her animal body,
wrapped in sweat and questions:
he is silent now,
whoever he is, no more
than the print of a jaw on the pillow,
a steady breath
like the wind above the roof
or the grass around her tower.

She feels herself
tipping into sleep, her own blood
buzzing in her ears. Now she dreams
she's back in the old yard: the patches
of black dirt, the fence, the swings,
the moon-white roses, her two
sisters in their starched skirts
hissing, whispering *no.*

3

Now is the time to look at Love:
now, as the clock gulps the hour,
she tiptoes over the groaning floor.
That monster, Love,

stirs his snaky length,
packed between pillow and blanket like midnight's masterpiece,
time's secret. Panicky, she locks her thighs
and lights her candle, raises her small flame high, high,

and the attic room cracks open like an egg:
black shapes, trunks, bureaus,
rolled up carpets, wicker chairs, rafters,
cobwebs, and a creaking bed,

and a man called Love on the bed,
who twitches awake as the wax
drips eyes of pain on his wrist, his chest, his forehead.
Still she bends closer, closer. If he is Love,

she is, after all, the Soul.
Now she glows like a candle herself,
translucent in her sex.
Is it morning now?

The great trunks shine like noon. He stares,
she stares. At last they rock with laughter, tremble,
couple and uncouple
in the new light.

SIMPLICITY

—For Elliot

Wishing to praise
the simple, the univocal, the one
word that falls like a ripe fruit
into an infinite well,
I watch

that easy old couple, limber
sixty-year-olds,
strolling, maybe just finished jogging,
under the plum trees.
Over their mild

gray heads the air
is pink with blossoms
accomplishing themselves;
under their tan, accomplished Keds
the sidewalk's pink with petals.

She turns to him and speaks, a word
that fills and falls like another petal,
easy, simple:
a word of thirst?—*milk? wine?*—
a word of love?—*good run?*—

whatever,
it befalls him
light as the stroke of a branch,
clear as color,
and he nods, smiles.

I want to learn that word, I want
to hold that word under my tongue
like a sip of milk,
I want to inhale that word
the way that gray-haired woman, now,

turns back to the tree
and inhales the lucid perfume
of a blossom that promises
ripeness, night, the sweetness
of the plum.

IN THE FOREST OF SYMBOLS

L'homme y passe à travers des forêts de symboles
Qui l'observent avec des regards familiers. . . .
                                    —Charles Baudelaire, *"Correspondances"*

I met you in the forest of symbols,
among roots, portents, etymologies.

You said *green*, and I became a blade of grass,
blue, and the sky swallowed me up,
red, and my shoes filled with blood.

I said *welcome*, and you shone like a new tulip,
goodbye, and you were midnight,
invisible, and you enveloped me like musk, like ambergris, like
        jasmine.

Ah, we were two eggs in the same nest
rocking on the black bough of meaning,
two feathers tipping the wing of the horned owl,
two pine needles piercing the great fog.

Love! we cried, interpreting the wind,
Rage! we screamed, *Significance!* we shrieked,
until our nest trembled and strange
axes hacked our words,

and the wild owl flew to a different woodland,
shedding us as she went.

BRAHMS: SYMPHONY #1

Dry drummings: drummings,
rain on the roof, falling gravel,
the gray landscape of Brahms,
heavy as a load of stone,
and the wind in the trees, a
peg-legged old conductor,

confers its tenor breath upon
black branches, creaking, complaining,
a heart in the ground, a beat
that's gone on too long.
And now we're traveling
through a granite tunnel,

wet walls, ferns, water
dripping, drumming, and our
ears rise like the ears of
cats in the dark, our eyes
shine. The conductor pauses. Brahms
is about to make his dark

announcement: darkness, he cries,
darkness, let there be
darkness. And there's a lake
of night. Middle age,
you sigh, middle age has
brought us to this.

But the air clears, whitens.
Dawn. Brahms waits
in clear air beyond the tunnel.
People are crossing bridges with
market baskets on their arms.
Geraniums growing in pots. Children playing.

Sun of the nineteenth century!
The old conductor smiles.
And hearts canter like fine horses,
gallop along the level street—
reins flashing, hooves loud—
loud, and gathering speed.

GLASS

In the land of glass
where everything is clear,
nothing is clear.

The glass roses chime in the sun there,
and the cabbage opens invisible circles,
bell within bell,

to the morning light.
The glass houses are hollow, wide,
whispers across still valleys,

and the shapes that move unknown from room to room
are shapes of the rainbow of animals:
the enigma of the giraffe

dazzles the walls;
the swan's feathers erase each other
over and over,

clashing like snowfalls;
the tongues of the snake
are glittering keys unlocking the floor.

There, my love, is
the land we're traveling toward.
There we too will be tough as shells,

no densities will harm us,
not the thickness of skin, not the softness of clothes.
And yet the sun and the moon

will see right through us,
and we'll no longer even try
to understand ourselves.

SITTING

--for Carole Peel

I assume the pose,
ring finger to temple,
the thoughtful subject,
eyes on a mythic distance.

Knife-keen pencil, square of blank light,
you begin, stooping, squinting, rearranging
my arms and yours, explaining
"It's so physical, so—so—"

No word comes: you laugh, shake your head,
bend to the space that wants to be filled, while
Mozart swarms around us, a hive of life.
"Music helps—"

Beyond your window
sun clasps the green lines
of a redwood—"so physical"—
I want to reach and touch

but the pose becomes me, holds me,
my body aches and stiffens, now
I'm passing out of myself,
now I'm spreading under your fingers,

my eyes darkening on the rough
sheet, your quick strokes
making me more severe until I look up
wondering how 'ou'll finish me

and see you're laughing, happy at how your pencil
cuts my mouth, just here
into a neat corner. . . .
Flat on the page, I stare, I stare.

Your ruffly white blouse, navy jeans,
black sneakers, yellow hair
strain through my sketchy
adjectives and nouns.

ON BLACK POINT BEACH

—For Marlene Griffith, who spoke

1

She said, *The door is open.*
She said, *You can go through.*

Sitting on the hot stairs, half down to the beach,
I see it for a moment—

no door at all but a wide
bright space, and beyond it

the place where something lives
that I must name:

                    two steep
arms of land, relinquishing

a giant motion, a drumming and fretting
that leaps, shines, spends itself

in halos of desire
that still are never spent, never done

shining or fretting
at the cliffs that

try to give them up
but can't.

2

Far above me is the meadow, solid as
history, the world you say is real, the thin
obligations of grass, the serious
responsibility of roots.

You want to keep me there, you
want my eyes to nail themselves
to objects, to the objectivity of
lumber and clay, of heavy classical angles.

But I want to tell you
(I keep on trying to tell you)
about this noise that
veils me, cradles me, enrages me,

these points of light in sand
that suck my vision up, these brilliant
gills of water, breathing
silence in and out.

3

A clear green wall comes in from the sea, over
and over announcing itself with drums, with thunder:
it's our own desire, always hastening

to close us in, always offering
a window on those distances where tiny ships
tremble along the edge of the world.

A crow clacks by, the meadow's emissary.
When I look up, following
its flat black flight

I see the mist that forms high up,
a cloth, a flag
that tells us what the ocean wants—

something to count on, something
to touch, something that stops
the long ache of the eye.

But if you visit me here,
if you sit here with me
for an hour while the sun is high,

our glances still will pass
through dazzle, through dizzy
layers of emptiness,

through the abstract blue
libido of the sea,
before everything

sighs, settles
down,
solidifies.

THE KITCHEN DREAM

4 A.M. We're making love in the kitchen, discovering
secret doors and windows in
the shadows behind the stove.

The refrigerator hums blessings, a complicitous
mother, guarding her great cartons of milk, her bins
of oranges, her dark pots of jam.

4:30. We hear the runners
pounding up the hill, we hear the birds
coming from the black oak,

and we say, Why go to bed, it's
almost dawn, and
our mouths meet, our fingers

unlock the silence, light
bathes the windows, and
we say, It's dawn,

we'll feed each other now:
and we open the heavy door,
saying,

Here are the pale cold eggs, the
bread, the coffee beans,
here are the oranges, still

flushed from the tree.

THE EMILY DICKINSON
BLACK CAKE WALK

1866:   Ned . . . inherits his Uncle Emily's ardor for the lie. My flowers are near and foreign, and I have but to cross the floor to stand in the Spice Isles. . . .

1883:   Your sweet beneficence of Bulbs I return as Flowers, with a bit of the swarthy Cake baked only in Domingo. . . .

—*The Letters of Emily Dickinson*

Black cake, black night cake, black
thick cake out of which Emily
leaps in bubbles of bitter sweetness—
lucid or dark balloons of Emily,
Emilie, Uncle Emily,
Dickinson, Nobody—
black Emily Dickinson cake,

how does your sugar grow?
What is the garden, where
is the furrow, whose
are the pods of heat and shadow?
How did black bulbs dissolve their iron,
leaves their silence, bees their drone of sunset honey
into the oven that cooked you firm?

Black cake, black Uncle Emily cake,
I tunnel among your grains of darkness
fierce as a mouse: your riches
are all my purpose, your currants and death's eye raisins
wrinkling and thickening blackness,
and the single almond of light she buried
somewhere under layers of shadow. . . .

One day I too will be Uncle Sandra:
iambic and terse, I'll hobble the tough sidewalks,
the alleys that moan *go on, go on*.
O when I reach those late-night streets,
when acorns and twigs
litter my path like sentences
the oaks no longer choose to say,

I want that cake in my wallet.
I want to nibble as I hobble.
I want to smile and nibble
that infinite black cake,
                                    and lean
on Uncle Emily's salt-white
ice-bright sugar cane.